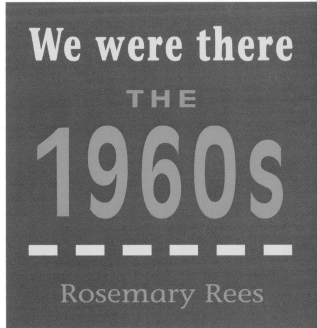

We were there

THE

1960s

Rosemary Rees

Heinemann

Heinemann Library,
an imprint of Heinemann Publishers (Oxford) Ltd,
Halley Court, Jordan Hill, Oxford, OX2 8EJ

OXFORD LONDON EDINBURGH
MADRID PARIS ATHENS BOLOGNA
MELBOURNE SYDNEY AUCKLAND
SINGAPORE TOKYO IBADAN
NAIROBI GABORONE HARARE
PORTSMOUTH NH (USA)

© Heinemann Library 1993

First published 1993
93 94 95 96 10 9 8 7 6 5 4 3 2 1

British Library Cataloguing in Publication Data
is available on request from the British Library.

ISBN 0 431 07330 9

Designed by Philip Parkhouse
Printed and bound in China

Acknowledgements
The author and publisher would like to thank the following
for permission to reproduce photographs:
Advertising Archives: pp. 7, 25
Barnaby's Picture Library: p. 14
Collections/Brian Shuel: pp. 4, 6
Con Dawson: p. 27; Hulton Picture Company: pp. 22
Robert Opie Collection: pp. 17, 19
Popperfoto: pp. 9, 12, 21, 28, 29
Joan Shuter: p. 30. Syndication International Ltd: pp. 15, 26
Topham: pp. 5, 10, 13, 16; John Walmsley: pp. 8, 11, 18, 23

Cover photograph: Hulton Picture Company

The author and publisher would like to thank all of the people who
contributed memories for this book.

Note to the reader
In this book there are some words in the text
which are printed in **bold type**. This shows that
the words are listed in the glossary on page 31.
The glossary gives a brief explanation of words
that may be new to you.

Contents

Home 1

Machines made housework easier in the 1960s. This kitchen has a twin-tub washing machine and a fridge.

Elizabeth Bown remembers her first washing machine.

We had been saving up to buy the washing machine for a long time. We bought it in May 1960, on the day that Princess Margaret (Queen Elizabeth II's sister) got married. I remember it was that day because I was a teacher, and schools had the day off to celebrate the wedding. So that was the day we had it delivered. I had to save up all my wages for two months to pay for it. It cost £82 8s 6d.

It was a Hoovermatic twin-tub machine. There were two tubs, side by side. You put the dirty washing and the soap powder in one tub, put down the lid and the machine washed for as long as you set it to wash, often only 3 or 4 minutes. Then you took out the hot, wet washing and moved it into the second tub, which spun it dry. You could use the hot water in the first tub to wash several lots of clothes. When you opened the lid the kitchen filled with steam!

Margaret Hudson remembers the new kitchen.

My mum went to the **Ideal Home Exhibition**, and she got her heart set on one of the new kitchens. The idea of a **fitted kitchen** was very new at the time, and she thought it looked as if it would be a lot less work. That's what she said to dad, but really I think it was all the shiny stainless steel and **formica** that she liked! Our kitchen just had a sink, a cooker, a fridge and a cupboard which had a flap that you used as a work surface. We also had a **pantry**.

So she ordered a kitchen, and the men came to put it in. We went out for the day, and when we got back it was still a mess, but by the end of the next day the kitchen was in. My mum was so proud. Everything was so new, and she had loads of space. Some of the cupboards were empty! She was very pleased with how much space it gave her. Our old kitchen table and chairs looked odd in the middle, though!

Not many people would have had a kitchen as modern and as big as this one. The cooker and the fridge and the gas rings are all built in to fit with the cupboards.

Home 2

A supermarket in 1962. Supermarkets sold a big selection of groceries, often more cheaply than the smaller grocery shops.

Fiona Grey remembers shopping with her mother in the 1960s.
At the beginning of the 1960s, we went to the shops several times a week. We visited all the different shops, like the grocer, the butcher and so on. We chose what we wanted, then they delivered it to our house later. Bread was delivered too, just like the milk. Sometimes my mum sent me to the shops to get things she had forgotten. It was friendly, all the shopkeepers knew you.

Then, early in the 1960s, my mum got a car. At the same time a supermarket, a 'Fine Fare', was built just a short drive away, at Hornchurch. After that we used to drive over there and get the shopping once a week. It wasn't as big as supermarkets are now, but it seemed huge at the time. It was strange to get a basket and help yourself to whatever you wanted off the shelves. It was also odd to do all your shopping in just one shop. It was quicker, but not as friendly.

Kate Upcott still remembers some of the adverts from the 1960s.
Because the TV was still quite a new thing to most of us in my school, we watched a lot of it. One **advert** that was very clever was the petrol advert 'Put a tiger in your tank', which was for Esso, and had a picture of a real tiger. It didn't just have a person telling you about the thing it was trying to sell. You could get tiny tiger tails to tie to the car aerials. Esso still uses the tiger in their adverts today.

Paul Shuter liked the songs that used to go with some adverts.
The adverts often had songs, and these songs were the sort that got stuck in your head and you just kept singing them. There was one song for carpet cleaning liquid that I can still sing today! Those are the ones I remember, but I don't think they made people go out and buy the things in the advert. Perhaps if you had to choose between two types of carpet cleaner you might buy the one in the song, though.

Advertising was used more and more in the 1960s, on the TV, on posters and in the papers. Many more people could afford cars like this Mini.

We wish you a merry Christmas and a happy New Austin

Austin Seven, 850 ccs 4 forward gears ■ THE AUSTIN MOTOR COMPANY LIMITED · LONGBRIDGE · BIRMINGHAM

School 1

Boys and girls, like the ones making models in this school, worked in groups at big tables. Not all the schools in the 1960s were run like this.

Rosamund Forbes went to several schools.

The school I went to in Oxford in about 1963 had boys and girls all mixed together, sitting around big tables. You could talk a bit as you worked. You were supposed to talk about the work, mostly. They sat the children who could read next to the ones who could not, so that they could help them along. You could not sit next to your best friends, or you would do nothing but talk!

Then we moved to Southport, and I went to a **convent** school. It was very different. There were lots of rules, and you had to wear a **uniform**. You were not supposed to talk at all, and the classes had lots of desks in rows, not groups of tables. They made much more of a fuss about getting things right, and you even had lessons to get you to speak 'properly', which meant in quite a posh voice. Mind you, the school dinners there were nice.

Children going out to play. In the playground boys and girls played different games. They sometimes joined up to play chasing games.

Rosamund Forbes played lots of different games at playtime.
We did a lot of skipping, with lots of different tunes to skip to. You started with simple skipping to 'salt, mustard, vinegar, pepper' then you went on to more complicated skipping songs where you did actions as well. Then there were skipping games where you jumped in and out of the rope with other people, jumping out on the month of your birthday, for example. As well as skipping, we played other games. Games like **cat's cradle**, with elastic around our legs – though I was never very good at that. There was a game called 'Mother May I?' where you were told to do something and had to remember to ask "Mother may I?" before you did it. We also played 'tig' and 'What's the Time, Mr Wolf?', which the boys could join in, and 'kiss chase', which they had to join in! Otherwise they were mostly off at their end of the playground playing football or something.

School 2

Some lessons were held outside. The children in the picture are travelling children who did not go to school. Teachers went to them.

Margaret Hudson went to school on the Isle of Wight.

My mum told me lots of stories about her school. It sounded horrible, with lots to learn and very strict teachers. The classrooms she was in were cold and painted brown. I wasn't very happy about going to school at all after these stories. I cried about it. But when I went, it wasn't like that at all. It was bright and colourful, and the teachers were young and friendly. You could sit where you liked, and you always had things explained if you didn't understand. We spent a lot of time outside in the summer. We had storytime out under the trees, on the edge of the school field. We also did lots of other work outside. I remember going outside with a hoop, putting the hoop on the grass and counting how many daisies were growing in the hoop. It was to help us guess how many daisies were growing in the whole field. I picked some to make the maths easier!

Rosamund Forbes enjoyed the end of the day.

At the end of the day, unless there was something special that needed doing, we always had a story on the carpet. I liked that time. You could sit with your friends, as long as you didn't mess about, and our teacher was really good at stories. If she read from a picture book then she held it up so we could all see the pictures. Some people made a lot of fuss about not being able to see the pictures properly. Our teacher also made up her own stories. There were no pictures for these, but she told us to close our eyes and try to see what was happening. They were such good stories that we didn't mind that there weren't any pictures.

We also sat on the carpet when she wanted us all to do the same thing. Most of the time we worked in groups. But if she was teaching us a song we all had to learn, or if she thought we all needed practice at something, then it was carpet time.

Most classrooms had a corner with a carpet where the whole class could sit for storytime, and when the teacher wanted to tell the whole class anything.

Work 1

A production line in a car factory. The cars moved along the line at a set speed, and the men stayed in the same place, doing the same job for each car.

Alan Clayton worked in a car factory in Cowley, Oxford.
The thing about the factory was that you were doing the same small job on a car each day. When we were making Morris Minor cars, 40 of them came along the **conveyor belt** every hour. You were paid by the amount of work you did. When you started, you could only fit a rear light. But with practice you could do the light and something else, then you got paid more. It was very noisy. Some jobs were very dirty.

The worst of it was that it was so very boring, doing the same thing all the time. So you talked to your mates, and didn't think about the work at all. You did that like a robot. The conveyor belt didn't stop, so each group of workers had an extra person who did your job for you if you needed the toilet. You had no time to fix things if they didn't work. There was a man called the 'reject man' who did that. The day shift was 7.15am to 12am. We had an hour for lunch, then worked until 4.30pm.

Women packing frozen chickens in a factory. More women went out to work in the 1960s, in factories, shops, offices, schools and lots of other places.

Rosamund Forbes' parents did not live together, so her mother had to go out to work.
My mum had a lot of different jobs, which needed to fit in around my school hours as much as possible. It was difficult for her, and she says that she lost several jobs because she had to stay home if I was sick. I don't really remember that. We moved from Oxford to Southport, then back to Oxford again, so she had to change jobs when we moved too.

The job she had that I remember the most was when she worked in a toffee factory in Southport, in 1965. The factory made toffee sweets called 'Penny Arrows', and she used to bring them home from work. She would give them away to all of my friends, who hardly ever had to buy sweets at all! She never let me have any of them, because she said that they would be bad for my teeth! I thought it was very unfair at the time. Now, I get quite cross when she gives my kids sweets!

Work 2

A secretary in the late 1960s. She is working from a tape-recorded set of letters, which her boss has dictated onto the machine. This was a new idea at the time.

Fiona Grey remembers training and working as a secretary.

I went to secretarial college in London in 1965. We all had to dress smartly, and were taught how to take notes in **shorthand** and how to type. We were taught to use **manual** typewriters, and electric ones, which were the latest invention. It was a long time before I ever got to use one when I was at work, most places couldn't afford them. I worked in offices, even when I was training. Once I worked in a bank.

Another girl and I stamped the first ever cheque cards in our area. I had lots of different jobs. Once I worked in a **solicitors'** office, and shocked them by coming to work in a bright orange and yellow mini dress! I went to university then, but did secretarial jobs in the holidays. Most of my work was still typing up notes I made of what my boss said. It wasn't until the end of the 1960s that we began to work from tapes. Not cassette tapes, but big machines, with big reels.

Mary Quant, photographed in 1960. She was one of the most famous dress designers of the 1960s.

Janet Withersby remembers the fashions at the time.

In 1965, when I was about 21, I went to live in London and shared a flat with two friends. **Mini skirts** were just becoming fashionable. We wanted to look fashionable. We really wanted to wear Mary Quant dresses, but they were too expensive for us, so we bought a sewing machine and made our own mini dresses. Skirts got so short that you could make a dress out of a square metre of material.

We had our hair cut in **Vidal Sassoon** bobs. Because my hair was curly, and the bob did not look right, I had to iron my hair through brown paper to get all of the curl out of it. It smelt awful when you were doing it!

On Saturday afternoons, we went to look in the windows of the shops in Chelsea, or in Carnaby Street. All the other girls we knew dressed in the same way. Some of the boys wore jackets like the ones soldiers wore.

Spare Time 1

A picture from the TV programme 'Thunderbirds'. It was very popular. Children ran around playgrounds shouting one of its sayings: "Thunderbirds are GO!"

Rosamund Forbes remembers early television.

We had one of the fairly early TVs. It was egg-shaped, and the screen stuck out quite a lot, like the back of a saucer. You had to put money into a meter to make the TV work. We had a bag of **sixpences** from the bank each week, and we had to choose what we watched very carefully. Watching 'Thunderbirds', for example, might have meant that there were not enough sixpences left at the end of the week to watch 'Sunday Night at the London Palladium'. I remember lots of the 'Watch with Mother' programmes, like 'The Woodentops', who were a family of wooden puppets. Their dog, Spotty, was always getting into trouble. Lots of programmes seemed to have puppets.

I liked 'Joe 90', which was like 'Thunderbirds'. But I thought that 'Stingray' was better, because it had a mermaid called Marina in it who I really liked.

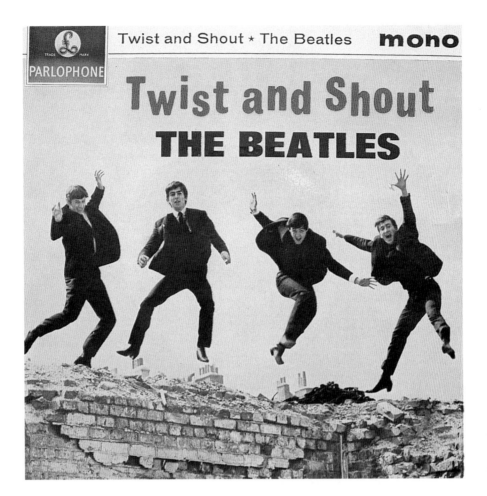

Twist and Shout ★ The Beatles **mono**

PARLOPHONE

Twist and Shout
THE BEATLES

The cover of one of the first Beatles records. The Beatles were one of the most popular groups of the 1960s, and were seen as really wild young men.

Pat Taylor remembers going to pop concerts.

I loved listening to the Beatles, but I never went to one of their concerts. I went to other pop concerts. I saw people like Billy J. Kramer and Cliff Richard. They were amazing, those concerts. They weren't held in huge places, like they are today, but in theatres or Town Halls. They seemed big at the time, though, because pop concerts were a new thing, and very exciting.

It felt so exciting to be there. You had to queue for ages, and sometimes you didn't even get a ticket. If you did get in, it was really hot, with everyone crammed in together. But that didn't matter. The person in the pictures on your wall was there on stage. Often it was hard to see them, but that didn't matter either. You could hardly hear the music! From the minute they came on stage until the minute they left, everyone was screaming with excitement. I was too.

Spare Time 2

A children's playground in the 1960s. The children are playing on a roundabout. There are swings behind them.

Jane Gross spent a lot of time in the playground near her house.
The playground near our house had a very high metal slide. It used to get very hot in the summer, so if you were in shorts or a skirt it hurt your legs. Going down got faster the more often people went down it, because they polished it with their clothes! When people had been going down all day, it got so fast that you could shoot right off the end! There were also swings, a see-saw and a wooden roundabout.

The roundabout had a ledge around the bottom, which you could stand on and push with one foot to get it to turn fast. The big boys were always pushing really fast until the little ones screamed, and we all thought the roundabout would spin off into space. You felt really sick and dizzy after a fast go on there. There wasn't any bark or anything for when you fell off, like in playgrounds today. If you were lucky, it was grass, but often it was concrete. That hurt a lot.

Bill Upcott and his friends all had Hornby train sets.

We all had Hornby train sets. They cost quite a lot of money, so we didn't have huge sets each. I had some track, and an engine that made a chugging noise and blew out steam. We all went to the same school and most days we would arrange to meet at someone's house to join all our sets together. That way we could make a big track, with lots of twists and turns and junctions. There were lots of bits of tunnel too.

We tried to make the track so that there was one main **junction** for all the trains. When we had done this, we all started our trains at different times so that they would arrive at the junction at the same time – and there would be a huge crash! It took a lot of practice to get it exactly right, but when we did, the crash was huge! Luckily, the trains were very well made. You could crash them over and over again without breaking them, or even denting them.

Some toys from the 1960s. There were not as many toys to choose from as there are today. But, compared to the 1950s, it must have seemed like children could have had anything they wanted.

Spare Time 3

In the 1960s doing silly things to make money for charity was very popular. These students tried to get as many people as they could into a Mini car.

Kate Upcott's brother was in a much more tiring stunt.

My brother and his friends pushed old pianos and sofas all the way from London to Brighton to make money for charity. That was nearly fifty miles (about 83 kilometres), I think. They took it in turns to push, and people promised to give them a few pence for every mile they did. My brother made it all the way, and was very proud of himself. He was very, very tired the next day.

Jane Gross went to another stunt involving pianos.

Our school set up a piano smashing contest at the end of the pier. There were six teams, and they tried to smash the pianos in the shortest time. They had to be smashed small enough for the bits to fit through a hole in the top of a big box. People paid to go and watch, and bought drinks and hot dogs. That was how the school made money. The noise they made as they smashed was really loud.

A girl on a scooter in the early 1960s. To begin with not many people could afford them, but they got cheaper.

Pat Taylor remembers riding on a scooter.

My **bloke** had a scooter, and we used to go off on it to the **seaside** as often as we could. You could go further away from home with a scooter. At the time, you thought the scooter was going really fast. Going off on a scooter was something that made you feel really daring, you thought you were it. You really had to hang on very tightly to the person driving, though, for there was nothing to keep you on.

Fiona Grey remembers her brother had a scooter.

My brother was older than me, and away at university. He got a scooter, which made him seem very grown up and glamorous. Because he was away most of the time, I didn't see that much of him. But I remember that once or twice, when he came home for the holidays, he gave me a ride on his scooter. I enjoyed that. We never told my parents, they would have been very cross.

Holidays 1

A group of mods going to Brighton. The mods and rockers went to seaside towns like Brighton and Skegness on Bank Holidays.

Pat Taylor remembers mods and rockers.

I was a mod, and I wore all the right clothes. It was like choosing sides, and you had to have the right clothes to show which side you were on. I used to go to the seaside with my boyfriend and lots of our friends, who were also mods. People used to say mods and rockers went looking for fights, but we just went for the day out. There were sometimes fights with the rockers, but I was never in one.

One year, in 1967, I was working in a gift shop in Skegness. It was a tiny shop, right on the seafront, and I was working there all on my own. It was Bank Holiday Monday, and some mods and rockers came on to the seafront. I thought that there was going to be a fight. I was very scared because, if there were fights, then the shops got broken up. It was odd to see ordinary people, just like the people you knew, get so angry and violent. I was lucky, the fight didn't happen.

Ice cream vans went the same way every day, so that children knew when they would come. They played a tune, so that they could be heard when they arrived.

Kate Upcott stopped at the ice cream van after school.

I had 2d (1p) for my bus fare home each day, and often spent it at the ice cream van. This meant that I had to walk all the way home. You could buy 'Rabbit's Ears' ice creams, with two chocolate covered pieces that looked like pointed rabbit's ears. We also liked 'Jubblies' which were triangles of fruit flavoured ice. You made a hole in the corner and sucked the juice out of one side, and then the other.

Paul Shuter saw ice cream vans in Sheppey and at the seaside.

Our ice cream van in Sheppey played a tune, I think it was 'Greensleeves'. It was always out of tune, anyway. It sold lollies and plain ice creams.

At the seaside, I remember there were ice cream trikes. The trike had a big box on the front, which had ice in it. You could only buy little blocks of ice cream with wafers to put on each side. I think a bell rang, so that you could hear the trike coming.

Holidays 2

A girl guide at camp. Going camping with guides or scouts was often the only holiday that many children had.

Kate Upcott was a girl guide in London.

I loved going to guides. They were very strict about your uniform, and about how you behaved. You had to iron your scarf each week before you went, and tie it just right. Now, my daughter Henrietta just puts on a sweatshirt – and she's ready!

Camp was really good fun. You had to do everything for yourself. Each group took it in turns to fetch the water, fetch the firewood, wash up (which we did standing on stones in the middle of a stream, in icy cold water), and clean out the toilets. The first camp I ever went to, our group put up the tent really carefully, and laid out **groundsheets** and sleeping bags just so. No-one told me that the groundsheet had to be just inside the tent. I had mine neatly just outside the tent. That night it rained. The rain collected on my groundsheet and I woke up at 2am soaking wet! Even that didn't put me off!

VENICE
14 DAYS FROM
£48.18s
ALL-INCLUSIVE

FUN SUN AND BEA

Fabulous Venice! How a BEA Silver Wing Holiday secures you 14 carefree days from only £48.18s all-inclusive

Holidays abroad were just becoming something that people could afford. They were much harder to arrange, as there were no 'package holidays' that did everything for you.

Paul Shuter went to France three times.

The first time we went to France was in 1966. We went to the South of France, and stayed in a holiday camp. We had a large room with beds for all the family, and everybody washed in the showers in the camp washrooms. You ate in one big dining area which had a roof but no walls. Everyone, except for the people who worked there, was British. Hardly any of them seemed to speak any French.

The camp was right down by the beach. The thing I liked most about the whole holiday, was that you could buy pancakes filled with jam down on the beach. A lady had set up a stall and she made them as you ordered them. I had never eaten jam pancakes before, and thought that you only eat pancakes on Pancake Day!

I ate egg and chips most of the time, although I think I could have eaten French food – I was just too fussy to try it!

Holidays 3

Many people could not afford to go away for a long holiday, at home or abroad. For many people a day trip to the seaside was their holiday.

Kath Donovan went on day trips to the seaside every year.

Every year we would go on a day trip to the seaside. We went by coach from Harlow shopping centre to Southend. We took buckets and spades, towels and swimsuits and sunglasses and hats in a big suitcase. I used to drag my Dad all the way to the coach stop every year, because I was so worried that we would miss the coach, or that it would leave early. We never did miss the coach.

Once we got to Southend, we made a camp on the beach. We played in the sea, and took turns to bury each other in the sand. You had to have just the right sort of sand, it had to be wet enough to stick together. The person being buried had to stay very still, or the sand would crack. If they got the giggles, you couldn't bury them. For lunch we always had fish and chips, then we went to the **amusement arcade** for the afternoon, until it was time to catch the coach home.

Rosemary Dawson's mother came to visit quite often.

My mum worked, and got two weeks holiday a year. She didn't go away on holiday, she came to visit us instead. It was a bit of a holiday for her, as she wasn't staying at home, but it wasn't like going to the seaside! She enjoyed it, though. It meant she saw us and, later on, Geraint and Thomas too. She helped in the house, so it was not as much of a holiday for her as going to a hotel would have been.

Bill Upcott went to stay with relatives too. This was during his school summer holidays.

My mother and I went to stay with **relations** in Guernsey one year. I think that it was some time around 1965. We spent a lot of time on the beach. I can only just remember this holiday, and I mostly remember it because it was very hot indeed. We have a few family photos of us taken on this holiday, they are mostly of people sunbathing!

Geraint Rees and his granny, in 1968. For many people going to stay with relations was the only way to afford a holiday.

Special Days 1

Bobby Moore, the captain of the England football team, being carried round the football pitch having just won the World Cup.

Paul Shuter was one of the many people who watched the World Cup Final on TV, in 1966.

In 1966 the World Cup Final was going to be held in England, at Wembley. It was held in different countries in each year. Because it was England's turn, there was a lot more fuss about it in 1966. There was a **mascot**, called 'World Cup Willie', a lion dressed in football kit. There was also a song about 'World Cup Willie'. The playgrounds were full of boys singing it. Everyone thought how good it would be if we won the World Cup in the year it was held at Wembley. The England team kept winning matches, and then at last they were in the final. They were playing West Germany, and everyone got very excited. On the day the match was played, it felt as if everyone was sitting around a TV somewhere watching it. Pubs hired TVs so that people could go there and watch the match. Everyone went wild when we won!

Stephen Vickers went to the pop concert on the Isle of Wight in 1964.

Pop concerts gave you a real feeling of sharing and friendliness. The Isle of Wight concert was for three days, but the travelling, unpacking and packing meant that the whole thing lasted about eight days. The travelling was all part of the experience. You would go loaded with tents and sleeping bags, and meet up with other people as you travelled along.

There was a lot of waiting around. None of the groups ever started on time. Groups and their equipment often got held up in traffic. You also had to queue for food and to use the toilets. But you talked to all sorts of people about the groups that were coming, and told stories about how long it had taken to get there! At the Isle of Wight Festival, the grocery shops ran out of food, and so everyone there just shared what they had with everyone else.

An open air Festival at Woburn Abbey. Festivals in the open air, most of which lasted for several days, were very popular in the 1960s.

Special Days 2

Bill Upcott built a snowman in his garden during 'the great snow' of 1963. It lasted a long time. There was deep snow everywhere, even on the beaches.

Paul Shuter was living on Sheppey in 1963.

It snowed for ages, and then the snow just stayed and stayed. Everyone was saying that the sea between Sheerness and Southend had iced over so that you could walk across. We didn't go to Sheerness until the snow had started to thaw. Then my mum took me and a friend of mine, called Mickey Fagg, to the beach. The beach was covered in snow, just like everywhere else. The sea wasn't frozen over but there were great chunks of ice floating along all the way across to Southend. They were huge, about eight metres or more across, and they looked very solid. They were moving fast in the current, though, and I think it would have been very dangerous to try to go across on them. We went home and built huge snowballs, as big as we were, in the garden. They were still there months later, after all the snow had melted and the ice had gone. We thought they would never melt.

Glossary

advert an advertisement, a picture or poster that is trying to sell you something.

amusement arcade a place where there were lots of machines that you put money in to play games. Today you can play video machines. In the 1960s there were different machines, which you worked by pressing buttons or pulling levers.

bloke a man. Pat says "my bloke", this means boyfriend.

cat's cradle a game which you can play with your hands, or with two people's legs, where you make patterns with a loop of elastic by threading it over itself again and again.

concerts singers give concerts where they sing their songs in a hall or other big place, sometimes outside. They charge people to come.

convent school a school that is run by nuns.

conveyor belt a moving floor which moves things along at a set speed.

day trip a visit to a place, just for the day. Coach firms and the railways ran day trips to places like the seaside.

dictation words spoken out loud so that another person can write them down.

fitted kitchen a kitchen where the cupboards and the other kitchen furniture, like cookers and fridges are all fitted together.

Formica a plastic covering for table tops and chairs, which can be wiped clean with a cloth.

groundsheets thick plastic sheets that you laid on the ground inside your tent when you were camping. They kept you dry.

Ideal Home Exhibition a big show, held every year, where people can see the most modern home furniture and designs.

junction a place where more than one road or railway meet.

manual by hand. Manual typewriters had no electric power to make typing easier. You had to hit the keys a lot harder.

mascot something which you think will bring you good luck.

mini skirts very short skirts.

mod in the 1960s there were people who called themselves mods. They wore fairly ordinary clothes, and rode scooters. They liked pop music. They did not like another group of people called rockers.

pantry a special room of the kitchen for storing food.

production line the part of a factory where something is made in stages. The item being made moves along in front of the people making it. Each person does the same job over and over again.

rocker in the 1960s there were people who called themselves rockers. They wore leather clothes, and rode motor bikes. They liked rock music. They did not like another group of people called mods.

seaside a place on the coast, next to the sea. When people talk about going to the seaside they often mean to a town by the sea.

shorthand a quick way of writing down words.

sixpence six old pence, worth 2.5p in new money.

solicitors people who work with the laws of the country. They help you to do things like write your will or sell your house without making any mistakes.

uniforms special clothes. Soldiers and nurses wear uniforms, some schools make their children wear them too.

Vidal Sassoon a famous hairdresser of the 1960s.

Index